of broken pieces and light ahead

by Christiane Karam

of broken pieces and light ahead

© 2022. Christiane Karam. all rights reserved.

published in the United States by the Unapologetic Voice House. the Unapologetic Voice House is a hybrid publishing house focused on publishing strong female voices and stories.

www.theunapologeticvoicehouse.com

no portion of this book may be reproduced, stored in a retrieval system, or transmitted in any form or by any means—electronic, mechanical, photocopy, recording, scanning, or other—except for brief quotations in critical reviews or articles, without the prior written permission of the publisher.

identifiers:
978-1-955090-10-0 paperback
978-1-955090-14-8 e-book
2021922217 Library of Congress number

illustrations and cover design: Noemi Cruciani

photography: Francesco Gargiulli

studio: BostonArtPassion

makeup artist: Seiko Kitagawa

to everything and everyone who prompted the words on these pages. you have taught me well.

table of contents

foreword vii
preface ix
acknowledgments xi
i look to the stars 1
sharp edges 2
your name glistens 5
voiceless 6
and there i was 7
a wave of love 8
blueberries 9
since the start 10
the painting 11
i should've known better 12
and here i thought 13
stefan 14
i am her...15
the hardest thing i ever had to do 16
our love showed up in my coffee cup 17
dear fear, dear shame.....................................18
prayer 19
oh, you..20
i loved to paint 21
it's been so long 22
hospitals 23
the more i practice 24

happy...25

not so fast, terror says 26

i miscalculated the distance 27

anatomy of a fighter 28

the 11th hour...30

i once saw a champion 31

you have to have carved 32

now on the other side 33

green tea 34

2am again...35

relationships 36

air pockets 37

blood family...38

my biggest regret..39

are you looking to live by yourself 40

four years...41

the last dream..42

you were the doorway...43

wilting...44

i am no stranger 45

queens, eagles, ...46

and here i was 47

crucified..48

friends 49

there are way too many others 51

the music lessons...52

so what if i feel?...53

sing along 54

covid...55

beirut 56

they're there 58

he was big 60

what i didn't tell you then.....................................61

ghosts...62

whirlwinds and voices..63

bassam 64

i own a ridiculous amount 66

lost and found 67

christiane 68

i'm going to turn you into a short story...................................69

the swan 70

he couldn't possibly want me...................................71

yesterday i started feeling 72

7 pm 73

ashes to ashes 74

the good girl 75

my mother's kitchen 76

your lips 77

the party 78

breathless 79

younger 80

heaps of kisses...................................81

turbulence 82

you and me 83

fall came early this year 84

mitochondria 86

guerres 87

peine 88

épave 89

هلّأ فلّيت 90

بتيجي على بالي 91

حنين 92

مين بقول 93

thay...................................94

about Christiane Karam...................................97

foreword

Ever since I heard Christiane read, at one of the first 'Writing from the heart' workshops she attended, years ago, I knew she was a writer; emotionally intelligent, articulate and compelling. Christiane has been healing pieces of herself and reclaiming her story her whole life, through writing, through singing, through the many facets of her voice. I hear the music in all her work. She's a truly original and incredibly powerful soul with a huge heart, a one of a kind human, and voice in the world, both as a writer and as an artist. 'Of Broken Pieces and Light Ahead' is a wistful, powerful and poignant work, a lifeline of exquisite reflections threaded together to inspire and comfort.

Nancy Slonim Aronie

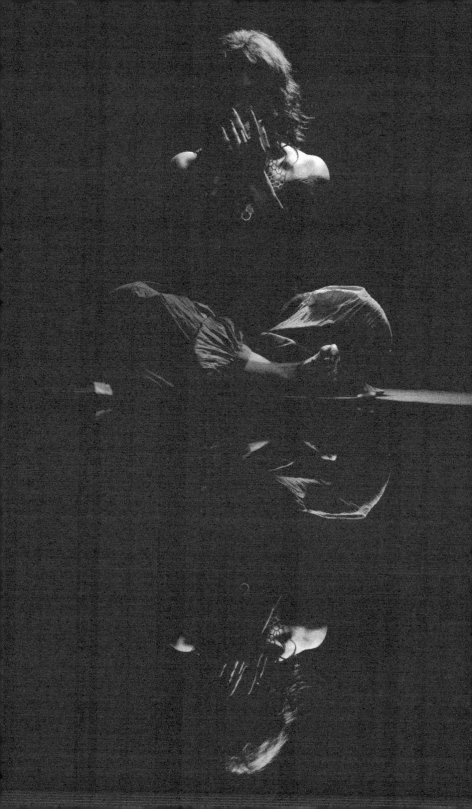

preface

it was a very long time ago, when i realized the magical power of words. something happened when i wrote. i felt better. and every sadness was lighter, as though naming the emotions and rearranging them in patterns helped release the heaviness. something about how words danced on a page gave me agency. in a war-ridden world where so much was out of my control, i could choose my words. and so i wrote. i must've been seven or eight when i began, and when books became a portal to endless adventures and sensations. and comfort. along with music, and in the midst of unfathomable violence, i had found my inner place of solace.

over the course of the past decade (or two?), i started collecting bits and pieces of moments i had put down on paper. moments of heartache, of grief, of joy. moments of rage, of quiet solitude, of terror. moments of bliss, of gratitude, of reminiscence, moments of wondering if i would ever be whole. and in my process of taking every leap of faith i found in me to take, i eventually did. and then covid happened, prompting further growth and further reflection. flashbacks became a thing again, and a sense of profound loss, but also of peace and clarity.

and so here it is, the journey, haphazardly documented in these short reflections. mostly in english, sometimes in other languages that are also part of my experience.

you will see that these snapshots don't follow any partic-ular order, chronological or otherwise. traumatic memory works in mysterious ways. one moment i'm inspired, in love, soaring, and the next heartbroken. one moment i am light, and the next thing i know, i am taken hostage by my old demons and sinking in the waters of terror again. but that is precisely the lesson. they are just moments. they come, they go, and in their aftermath, alongside the tears, and the laughter, more grounding, a new perspective, and freshly arranged words, awaiting their chance to become a portal for new possibilities. for inspiration, for courage, for fortitude.

acknowledgments

it took the proverbial village to make this work manifest.

first and foremost, eternal gratitude to my mentor and dear friend, Nancy Aronie, whose incredible book 'Writing From The Heart' rocked my world the minute i set foot in the United States, almost twenty four years ago. it is no coincidence that i found myself in her workshop, many years later, determined to find my writing voice, only to realize it had been there all along.

and then there was Tracy White, whose valiant spirit moved me and who even in the throes of terminal illness, found it in her to connect me to Carrie Severson; who instantly loved this manuscript and took me on as one of her authors. no coincidences.

and then i met Noemi, whose exquisite illustrations brought the stories to life in more ways than i had thought possible. and then came Francesco, with his uncanny ability to capture my soul with his photography.

many more beautiful writers, teachers and readers graced this path, providing feedback, and prompts, and tissue; too many to list here but i trust you know who you are. shout out to Amy Ferris, Blair Glaser and Sherry Amatenstein especially, whose workshop 'Women Writing To Change The World' provided a valuable framework at a particularly raw time in my process.

and last but not least: so many of the people i have loved are in these pages. so many of whom i know loved me deeply, too. family, friends, lovers. i thank each and every one of you, for the lessons, the songs, the growth. for the magic, the memories. for the courage to dance, to trust, for the beauty. so much beauty in daring to love. and wisdom, and compassion, after the heartache has taken its course.

fragile and clumsy and mighty as we may be on this shared adventure of life, we are all still learning.

i look to the stars

and i can hear you in one of them. they each remind me of
how much i have loved. how lucky am i to walk under such
a brightly lit sky.

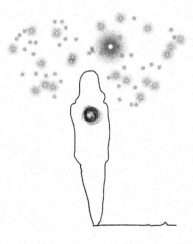

trauma. a word filled with so much grief, darkness, devastation. but also, comfort, ease, and the relief of having a home, somewhere, no matter how wretched.

i was a war survivor for the longest time. a war child, as some liked to call me.

and i seemed broken. for so long.

war had taken the frail insides of the terrified child that i was, and forever fragmented them into what felt like a trillion dark and dangerous pieces that all stung and that i could never put back together, no matter how hard i tried. they were sticky and rusty and made my heart bleed every time i tried to hold them. they had sharp edges and black holes in between. gaping wounds of grief and horror. doors impossible to shut. life impossible to birth.

fast forward to a transcontinental move and the belief that i still had a shot. it took all the courage i had in me to take that leap. i had been faced with the choice to live or to die. so many had not even been asked. but here i was.

what was it going to be? i found myself slowly but surely breathing my way into living. there were many tears yet to be shed. many frozen memories to still face and attempt to melt. but how did one go about melting these hardened walls that encased you inside your unfathomable past?

there was so much to learn about the simple business of living. many others seemed to be going about it pretty well. i had watched them growing up. i had watched them on TV, from my bunker. i saw how their lives were nothing like the life i was living. they woke up every morning, with, or so it seemed, very little or no fear of not waking up the following day. they had power, they had phones, they had running water, they went to work, they went to parties. they wore fancy things and they laughed and laughed and their eyes sparkled. the sky was blue where they were and the birds weren't afraid to fly. i wanted to be like them, now that i had the chance, but how did they do it? did they not smell the stench of death everywhere they went? i smelled blood just going down the street, not because it was there, but because my brain kept telling me it was still there. did these people not fear being maimed by shrapnel or landmines or the sheer cruelty of fate? but i wanted to live, i wanted to learn, i wanted to love. i wanted to feel joy in my body and not just at the movies. i still didn't know how. the little bubble in my head had always saved me growing up. it was a place i went to where i could be safe and where i could create a happy world. but my body never came along. it didn't know how. my body had learned it was always in danger of being blown up so it didn't believe in a happy world, it just never came along.

that seemed fair enough for a while. after all, for a traumatized person, i was doing really well. i was a war survivor and that's what we did. but that story no longer felt very good. it had been very comforting for a long time, as though it granted me shelter when nothing else fit. it was a good place for my homeless soul, constantly teetering between before and the afterlife, never quite here, or quite in this moment. but now i wanted it all. i wanted to sing and dance and fill my cells with life, all of them, all the time. so i kept at it, i kept poking at the fear, at the holes, i kept singing my shaky voice into my truth until it could roar. crying the trillions of tears into the trillion pieces until the walls started to break down and sunlight started peeking through from the cracks within, until my body could dance, fully trusting that fate was on its side.

and where i find myself today, there are no others. here we are, all survivors of one war or another, all just being the light that we can, every day that we can. and trauma, a dear old friend, framed in gold in the back of my mind, honored for the many lessons it taught me, and the ever so humbling reminder of what a magnificent sunrise a little love, courage and unwavering faith, can make of a trillion broken pieces.

your name glistens

over everything
your eyes color my sky
how full my heart is to have known you
how light it feels to no longer ask why
and simply let it be,
deliriously joyous to find us still dancing.

voiceless

silence
the monsters are back
roaring from all around
threatening to take your soul
hush hush
not a sound
the dragon's awake
and its wrath so near
lips sealed
as your words dance before your eyes
muffled songs of war and grief
and your hands color
and your heart cries
in silence.

and there i was

picking up the pieces, dusting off my pants, scraped
knees and all. one last look behind my shoulder. one
last glance at the carnage that had just taken place in
my heart. and then onwards. on the path. until the next
breathtaking moment of magic. or the next heartbreak. in
the meantime, just keep walking.

a wave of love

comes crashing in
with all its might and beauty
leaving you drenched and grateful, breathless,
enlightened
but then the wave pulls back
as waves do
and leaves you empty
hungry for more,
for more light
more breathlessness
more might
more gratitude
but it's gone,
yet the gifts it bore
are already in you.
how do you stay put
how do you stand still
and feel it pull away
while holding the love
and the might and the light
and the breathlessness
so wide open
that it is now eternal
resting in the palms of your hands?
how do you not give way to fear
how do you trust that there will be another wave
how do you trust that you don't need another wave
that its beauty and its might and warmth and light
are forever a part of you
and that every breath you take
can now be life giving?

blueberries

blueberries, blueberries everywhere
and not a thought to bear
blueberries for days, months, years
blueberries forever but will i still be there?
blueberries hiding, blueberries hugging
blueberries waiting for the storm to pass
blueberries frozen, and my lips turn blue
blueberries so ripe and sweet but still the world is ending
the world is grieving, the world is choking, the world is
gasping for air
the air that never came, years and years of pretending
and now our lungs are caving
sirens everywhere, makeshift masks, makeshift morgues
ventilators, respirators, but the dams have broken
quick, more blueberries, cold and numbing
so many thoughts, so little time
the world is choking and so am i
blueberries frozen and my lips turn blue
will i ever breathe again?

since the start

of covid-19,
i find myself packing
packing my insides, packing my outsides, packing
sifting, sorting, tossing, just packing.
shelves and boxes fill my mind
and also my apartment
what will i need if i stay, what comes with me if i go,
who do i call when i'm on my way?
memories come flooding back, of good times and hard
times
boy were the hard times hard,
they still fill my eyes and rattle my soul if i let them
but the good times always take the cake,
so i let them
the laughter, the hugs, the joy, the love, the trips, the
smiles,
the stories, the moments, the treats, the kisses.. lots of
kisses
the i love yous, the i'm sorrys, the mountains, the trails,
the sea
the songs, the sounds, the colors
so much love, so much heart, so much joy in every
moment
so many moments, such bounty, so much bliss
all here, alive, still, in this very breath, vibrant and enough
this must've been what they meant when they said 'travel
light'
here it is then, the light of the world, right here in the
palm of my hand
i'm ready to take flight.

the painting

peacefully she slept under my painting,
with the cat at her feet,
the ghost of me hovering over her head
while she dreamt tenderly in his bed,
that he would forever be hers
two years later, she's gone and no more bed
the dream, the thrill, the kill, all came and went
the ghost of me still hovering over their heads
the cat has gone too and innocence has died, we have all
lost at this miserable ride
where is my painting i wonder, and where is he now?
our dream is dead
while i forever hover over his head.

i should've known better

than to stay in the darkness, and believe it for so long.
to take in the violence, unrelenting, raging, inside and
outside, day after day, year after year.
i should've known better than to quit every time i was
brave enough to start something, and was called names
and told i couldn't.
i should've known better than to get my lungs sick so i
didn't have to sing, to hurt my body so i didn't have to run,
to silence my dreams so i didn't have to speak.
i should've known better than to wait for the words that
never came, to sit with them at that table until i couldn't
swallow, to cut myself time and again so i could forget the
pain.
i should've known better than to starve so i could
disappear, and bury myself next to the dead so death
could not find me. i should've known better.

but my sweet child, i didn't. and while i can't go back and
undo my unknowing, i know that i know better today. you
are safe now, will you walk with me?

and here i thought

the world was a safer place because you're in it.

stefan

a twig, a branch, a tree
a drum, a stick, a key
many a night and day
counting, practicing, clapping,
singing, laughing, playing
sharing moments, sharing stories
love stories, life stories,
bridging time zones, always caring
and the audience roaring
and the last dance, and the many plans
and that bottle of wine you had saved
that we were going to drink in Spain
so soon, and now, never
a twig, a branch, a tree
a drum, a stick, you're free.

i am her

beautiful. but broken. wanting you to pay attention, to care, to put her first. wanting you to want her. breathless, like you did in the beginning. to change, to grow, to stretch, just so you can love her more.
i am her. waiting, hoping, grieving. waiting some more, hoping some more. maybe tomorrow you'll write. maybe tomorrow you'll call. maybe tomorrow you'll get on an airplane and tell her you love her and she'll be the one who gets to win your heart and keep it.
i am her. broken and awake. broken and asleep. broken and paralyzed. why were we not enough? i am her. my body remembers. how you pulled away. how you didn't want to touch me anywhere. how you looked at me with cold distant eyes. how you cringed everytime i tried to come close. how i cried myself to sleep in the other room, gutted, with no more dreams to keep me safe.

i am her, pretty but empty. angry, enraged. did we ever matter? i am her. is she me? how many more will there be?

the hardest thing i ever had to do

was believe you when you said goodbye.

here i am, years later, unbroken, again. whole, again.
standing, again. restored from the millions of tears shed,
the gut-wrenching pain of my heart literally dissecting, the
endless breathless, sleepless nights, gasping for air and
for any and every shred of hope i could hold on to. years
of rebuilding myself, my life, my faith, years of successes,
of achievements, of accolades, of transmuting grief into
growth.
but the fault lines remain. and fault makes everything
harder.
so go, my sweet little prince, my light, my knight, my
friend, my sun, my joy.
seek, stumble and soar. far away from me, but in my
bones, always.

our love showed up in my coffee cup

bleeding and beautiful as can be,
soaring through the skies and wounded as we are
frozen somewhere between yes and no
surrender and resistance,
joyous and tormented souls.

our love showed up in my coffee cup,
red and bold and burning through the cold
longing to be embraced,
waiting for the pain to turn back to gold
and for our i don't knows to stop fearing
the other side of the road.

dear fear, dear shame

dear doubt, dear guilt, dear terror:

i know you kept me safe when all i had was you. i know we
know each other inside out, and that you kept me quiet
and alive for a very long time.
and i know we had a deal. i got to survive, and you got to
make me pay for it.
but i'm all paid up now. i am ready to step into the light.
i'm not entirely sure who i can be without you but i know
i'm finally ready to find out.
i know you'll be visiting, and i know that every once in a
while, i'll be too tired to keep you at bay. but that's ok. i
know that even then, you won't be able to take hold for
too long. i know you'll sneak in every time i have to go
on stage, or want to publish my art, or get in the ring, or
say something important to someone. or to the world. my
mind will race, my stomach will hurt, and i'll think i'd rather
die than show up for myself. but that's ok. we've been
doing this dance for a little while now.
you know you can't silence me anymore. thank you for
everything you've taught me. i'll take it from here.

prayer

what is it that i'm not wanting to hear?

where is it that i'm not wanting to go?

oh, you

decades and just a second ago you were making love
to me. or was it in the next second. everything the same
and everything different. everything said and everything
unsaid. so very done and yet. it's all here. still.

i loved to paint

i loved to read and write. i loved to sing. i loved to play.
bombs raging outside, no dreams to be had. except the
colors on the page. and the songs. and the stories i could
disappear into.
but math awaited. and science. and all the other things
everyone else seemed to so effortlessly be doing. the
numbers, the facts, the certainties. the safe and secure
and lucrative. so confusing, so cruel. who was i? all i
wanted to do was color over a world engulfed in flames.
all i wanted to do was sing my song to the mother
shrieking outside my window who had just lost her child.
'you have the brains to be a surgeon and you want to sing?
you want to paint?' never mind, i thought. i was nobody
and nowhere to be seen, might as well be engulfed in
flames.

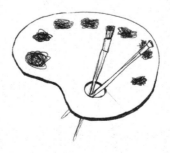

it's been so long

since i've written anything

so many stories have come and gone. so many ups, so
many downs. so many maybes, so many i don't knows.
waiting to get on stage to hopefully share some magic.
to be a vessel, to convey some light. to forget about the
betrayals, the heaviness, the shortcomings. all the ways
you and many i choose to hold close, make me question
my purpose every day.

and every day i have to choose all over again. to be happy.
to not need any of you to show up any differently than
you do. to not let anything or anyone steal my joy. to keep
my eyes on the prize. and my heart on the dream. and my
voice in the magic. to accept the invitation and embrace
all that is holy, every moment, to cup the sacred in my
hands.

i'm finally strong enough to look out for myself without the
comforting of another.

on i go.

hospitals

long nights, lying awake, on a hospital bed. struggling
to breathe. the beeping machines signaling along. the
comforting sound of the nurses hustling and bustling in
the hallway, tending to the floor. here for my every need.
so many stays, so many nights, sometimes needing the
care, and at times providing it, years ago, to the countless
casualties of war, maimed and forever changed by the
horror. within these sacred walls, everyone knows things
don't always turn out well. not everyone will still be here
tomorrow. pain is in the air, families are praying, hoping,
grieving, souls are transitioning, energy is moving, love
is all that matters. a safe place of courage and fortitude,
always in my heart.

the more i practice

the more i understand.
and embrace the solitary nature of all things.
in that space dwell our gods and our demons, our
questions and our answers, our nothings and our
everythings.

communion then becomes the sacred and ever so elusive
relinquishing of all that keeps us from ourselves and
others; the blissful coming together of solitudes that have
learned to dance in the dark.

happy

light. balance. joy. singing. breathing and walking in a city
i love. can't believe i'm on the other side of terror.

not so fast, terror says

the desolation of war is not too far behind nor might it be too far ahead. someone you love is at this very moment with someone else and a close friend you thought you could trust has just turned on you. you are under the weather and there's a war raging outside your door between your housemates. you need another place. but first in the midst of all this you have to find a way to birth your voice and open your heart so you can sing tonight. new project, new gear, new risks. what if the ideas don't come? what if the gear falters? what if the harmony sucks? and it's all being filmed. and they're ALL going to be there.

'but darling', i heard myself say, ' you ARE ready. as a matter of fact, that's exactly what you have signed up for. the whole thing. the foreplay and the fun. the cramps, the crippling thoughts, the obligatory pangs of anxiety. the ifs and the whethers it would've been better to pass this one up. the ifs and the whethers you should be singing at all, or improvising, or composing, or teaching, or boxing, or writing, or whether you're really any good at all at any of it. that's precisely the point darling. to enter this tunnel of doubt every single time you stand a chance at anything good, and come out of it victorious, every single time, because the light of your showing up was enough all along to lift everything else up. so go ahead, tremble, show up and shine. this is what you do, this is what you have come for. and this is what we need from you so we can awaken. don't let us down.'

i miscalculated the distance

between us and found myself simultaneously trapped
and lost in a pitch-black valley, far from you, but most
devastatingly, far from me. years later, i have found my
way back to solid ground and i can no longer see the
plains in which you roam. only shadows remain, floating in
the distance, where once shone a light brighter than the
sun, my dream of you.

anatomy of a fighter

breathe
regulate
pain
breathe
regulate
sting
breathe
regulate
keep moving
blind
breathe
jab
regulate
keep moving
crack
breathe
keep moving
regulate
i can do this
I can do this
bam
i can do this
I will do this
i can't breathe
breathe
jab
find the opening
find the airway
protect yourself

breathe
all the way in your back
you got this
one more round
keep standing
breathe
ouch
you're going to be ok
keep moving
keep standing
keep breathing
keep punching
hands up
protect yourself
you got this

30 seconds
all out
you got this
almost done
time!

the 11th hour

motherfucker
motherfucker
you motherfucker
motherfucker
tears of rage
there it is
the rage
finally
the abscess is breaking
let it all out
the rage
the anger
the disappointment
let them fly
motherfucker
how dare you
motherfucker
fuck you
lying son or a bitch
fuckin wuss
how dare you
here it is
in your face
thank you for the lesson.

i once saw a champion

fall.

it was not pretty. unmistakable. she fell. on the ice. as the world watched. thousands of hours of preparation. her reputation. her sense of self. her hopes and dreams. all fell with her. and the whole world held its breath. as she got up, and finished her dance. and then she waited. her head high, her eyes full. a million thoughts racing through her head. about who she was. who she thought she was. who she would now probably never be. she was a champion. how could this have happened?

the raging crowds outside her head were quieting down. the thoughts were slowing down. she got a few hugs. wiped a few tears. took a deep breath. and back on the ice she went. she was a champion.

you have to have carved

enough space inside yourself to know how to receive a
love this big. and you didn't have that space. and you just
didn't know how. when will i stop feeling betrayed by your
rhythm is the only question my heart hasn't answered yet.

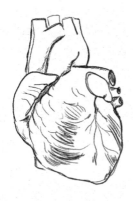

now on the other side

of the madness.

breathing again and waiting for it all to settle. for the
picture to get clearer. and the choices kinder.

green tea

and honey. green tea and honey. kept me alive. kept my
hands warm and my heart beating. when all the rest of
me was sobbing, blinded by grief. when all of me was
on the floor, in knots of pain and terror. days and nights
and weeks and months. green tea and honey. so sweet,
so soothing, so grounding. my friends, my keepers, my
connectors to reality, my welding to this earth. thank you.

2am again

eyes closing time on this side of the world. while on the other, yours open. nothing has been the same since august 11, 2013. or june 24, 2014. or february 1, 2015. or august 9, 2016. and yet it's still 2am every day here. and 9am where you are. nothing is the same and everything is the same. only half of me is here, and the other half is with you. half of me is on the east coast, in my music, in my body, in my head, in my life. and the other half is with you, walking down the streets of your city that i love, holding your hand, riding in your car, singing along to music, waiting for you to come back from your gig so we can snuggle and go to sleep. or maybe make love, or maybe giggle till dawn. nothing has changed and yet nothing is the same. a trail, visible only to me, takes me all the way there, where the grass has grown above my grave and is green as can be. a conduit that keeps pulling back. but back to what? hundreds of days and nights, of kisses and new friends and conversations have painted over the last molecule of what was us. so much has changed and so much is still the same. when will it end?

relationships

come and go. change is constant. am i ready to love you
in a way that allows you to be who you are? to love you
how is good for you? am i ready to love you in a way that
doesn't hinder your growth? that is not controlling and
fearful? that is not stingy and small? am i ready to do what
i've been expecting from you all along?

air pockets

in their neck.

calluses on her fingers. bruises on their body. strong
arms that can hold the instrument, fists that can stun you
blind. extraordinary hearing abilities. sharp eyesight and
dexterity of the fingers. coordination. flow. primal instincts.
heightened pattern recognition, power punches and
battle scars. thousands of hours on end of preparation
for one minute of transcendence. or demise. we have all
grown in the very specific ways we have chosen to make
our mark in this world. like tracks. or circles in the trunk of
an ever wisening tree.

blood family

and family blood.

an end and a beginning. a beginning and an end. red
blood flowing from your broken open heart. a dark and
gaping hole calling me to follow, always.

and now, years later. i'm still here. you would've been
45. maybe an artist. with a couple of kids. lots of
laughter. and hours on end in that dark room, developing
photographs behind those thick glasses that helped shield
you from our violent world. we could've been friends.

my biggest regret

was giving you my heart.

your biggest regret was losing hers.

there was nothing to end, we had never even begun.

are you looking to live by yourself

or with roommates?

with roommates is fine. 43. divorced. broke. and reeling
from my biggest heartbreak to date. hello again NYC.
ready to pick up this dream where i had last left it off.
before my life and heart shattered into a million pieces.
again. let's see what we can do with the fragments this
time.

four years

thank you for the revolution.

i can finally turn my face to the sun now
i can finally see that you're only a shadow
still here but no longer keeping me from the light.

the last dream

drawings on the wall
red and green
you replaced the one i liked best
and got some more
and once again i found myself wondering
why you didn't think of getting me one
and if you were going to kiss me
instead i waited and waited
like before
like always
like never again.

you were the doorway

to the hell that was to save me.

wilting

everyday i woke up to the sounds of the world ending
crashing in on our little souls
and to that familiar voice
that kept saying
i was wilting
without having lived
or loved,
wilting away
forever wasted
forever unyielding.

i am no stranger

to chronic pains.

you will just be one of them. good days and bad days.
smooth days and bumpy days. flares and moments of
respite.

breathing, still.
joyous, still.

queens, eagles,

witches and goddesses.

they just fly.

and here i was

finally closing the door shut. quietly. firmly. irrevocably.
on my longing. my never ending, heartbreaking, soul
crushing black hole of a longing. for closure. for love. for
attention. for amends. for everything i wished could've
been different. for every dream i believed would unfold.
for every embrace i lived a thousand times in anticipation
of what was to maybe come. for every wound i hoped
could heal. for every painful memory i wished undone.
for magic to inhabit once again the songs that now
only brought tears. for every lie that i prayed could be
redeemed. but it turns out you were the lie. you were
the hallucination, the life-threatening addiction and the
saddest joke. and now it was definitely on me.
a few more tears, a chuckle and a shrug. and i'll be on my
way. sometimes it takes being blind to learn how to see.
now on the other side of this storm of storms, i can finally
look towards where joy awaits. so goodbye, beloved door
behind which roam my fears, ill-fated hopes and stillborn
dreams. i'm turning my back on you. you have served me
well.

crucified

buried under the rubble
and the names
and the faces
of all who didn't make it
why not me
why them
what is the way forward
and what will it keep costing
day in and day out
one haunted night at a time
to stay here when they have all gone?

friends

'i'm picking her up at the mall at 6pm.
  i suppose you'd rather not meet her?'.
'of course i'd love to meet her, i said, why wouldn't i? let's
go.'
we had been running errands that day- because by then,
it was apparently obvious to the entire world that we'd be
better off as friends. he parked in front of the building and
we silently went up the escalator to where she was waiting,
my stomach steadily cramping along.
this beautiful smart young woman he had once assured
me he didn't envision having anything serious with had
now moved in with the love of my life. and i couldn't feel
my legs.

there she was. 'so good to finally meet you, i've heard so
much about you!' 'you too!' hug, kiss.
'i'll be right back', she said.

'oh she's just a little nervous', he commented.
'why is she nervous? what did you tell her?'
'oh you know, just that we had a thing'.

my insides were now screaming, as i stood there in
disbelief, legs shaking, vital organs hard at work to keep
me upright and poised. my world was falling apart, and i
had just been put away on a shelf in a small box that read
'a thing'.

she came back and they proceeded to shop. it was the day after new year and they were looking to decorate their new found bliss. 'oh i love the color! oh look it's on sale!' as she handed him a holiday candle to smell.

happy new year, she said, as they both hugged me one last time before walking back to the car. one last costly smile before i turned around, tears running down my face and into the first coffee cup i could grab onto. i sat there for a while, staring at the ripples until i finally pulled up my phone, and called my best friend, eyes blurred and heart shredded to pieces:
'he loves her, she's pretty. what do i do now?'

there are way too many others

who feel the exact same way as i do. i don't belong in a
crowd of heartbroken women.

an aberration. so much beauty. and devastation. a kind teacher, a little frantic, a little flustered by the chaos outside. would she be able to go back to her family today? would the checkpoints allow it? or the raids?

she snapped sometimes. 'you played the wrong note! can't you see?'
i tried to see. i tried to hear. i loved Chopin. he too knew war and exile and the perils of homelessness in his own land.
he too knew the life-saving absurdity of music in the dark pit of terror. he too knew illness.
his lungs did not survive the heartbreak.

years later, my lungs would choke too. grief is indeed a stubborn companion. thank God for the music.

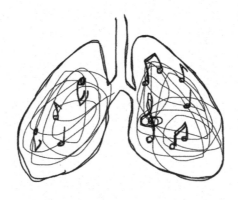

so what if i feel?

so what if i remember, so what if my heart has not forgotten? so what if every song is seared into my being, along with every moment i thought i could fly and the countless moments i almost died? so what if it's all still here except you? so what if maybe you never really were? so what if what you're after keeps taking you further and further away from me? so what if i believed and i was wrong? so what if we should've never met at all? so what if i no longer know who i am, now that i don't have you to remind me?

i couldn't breathe. i hated them. all of them. loud. brutal. obnoxious. strangers.
as i looked out the car window, crammed as i was on the left side of the narrow backseat- my siblings to my right, kicking and screaming, and my parents in the front. arguing. or talking. or arguing.
i struggled to hold back my tears. i swallowed everything that wanted to come out of me. again. all the shards of glass i wanted to spit in their faces. again. they were now ripping my insides. again.
i wanted that song. i NEEDED that song. there was a reason it had come on. just for me. just at that moment. i needed it to muffle the violence everywhere. i needed it to keep me from drowning. i needed it so i could sing along and pretend i was not in hell.

i begged.i pleaded. i cried. to no avail. in one resounding click, the radio was turned off. yelling was more important. the song was probably over by now. and all that remained were shards of glass. and tears that wouldn't stop.
and there had gone another day, just like that. another dream, another gaze. out the window.

covid

the year it all ended. or maybe the year it all finally began.
where had i been all this time? jetlagged, burned out,
hopping around the planet like there was no tomorrow.
and now that there WAS no tomorrow, the hours seemed
to slip away a little less furiously. twenty-four hours a day
NOW felt like enough time to process, to feel, to get work
done. to eat well, to sleep enough, and to be here. to
take in the heartbreak, and sit with it. until it revealed us
to ourselves. until it told us where it wanted us to go. what
it wanted us to hear. where had it been hiding this whole
time? in my belly. in our underbelly. years. decades. a
lifetime of pretending all was well with the gaping wound
of this earth. until its fury swept over us and left us all
gasping for a better tomorrow.

perhaps now was finally the time.

beirut

where i come from
everything is deadly
everything stings
bites
cuts
everything bleeds
cries
everything hurts
shrieks
convulses
crumbles in despair

where i come from
we revolt
we rebel
we try
we want to live
we build
we rebuild
we believe

we stand
we rise

until we fall again

where i come from
everything dies

where i come from
living is dying

and no one will ever know

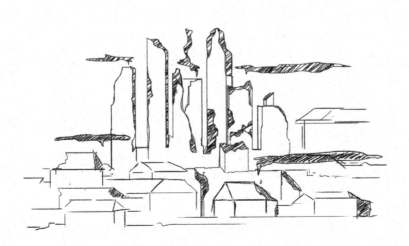

they're there

they're giggling. i hear them talking about a time and a place. where are they going? i come closer. they barely notice and proceed to disperse in pairs and threes. they walk, they talk, their steps and voices fading in the distance.

clearly there's a plan, clearly it's a big night. clearly i missed something. again. i'm in the outer circle. again. on the outskirts of my very life. again.
invisible. again.

the party's so very loud. everyone's having so much fun. they're all there. every single one of them. and i'm here. in the dark. deafened by my own inability to speak up. to stand for myself. to go. to be. to connect. to enter the circle.
but i don't know how.

tomorrow they'll be giggling again. sharing stories, blushing and gushing at the boys they kissed. tomorrow i'll watch them live and love and laugh and share and connect and be a circle.

and i'll be standing here. alone. on the outskirts of my life. choking. again. silenced by an invisible hand around my throat. deafened by my breaking heart's longing to belong.

will i ever know how?

he was big

fierce. tender. strong arms. warm eyes. a champion of
champions. always there to help, support, lend a hand.
make you better and stronger.
he was strict, but kind. he liked to laugh. i thought of him
fondly, and often. something about his presence quieted
my soul wherever i went.
i could see by the tattoos on his body that he had
traveled a harsh road. or had he? why so much ink, why
so much pain? what had thousands of needle pricks
failed to silence? what demons still lurked underneath
this beautifully painted skin? what terror still inhabited
this exquisite mountain of perfectly chiseled and slightly
intimidating muscles? what dreams still longed to sing
behind the armor?

he liked bright colors. so did i. he loved to help people.
so did i. he kept a distance. so did i.
i felt safe when he was around, perhaps because the
lonesome warrior in me had recognized the lonesome
warrior in him.

we had both built fortresses around our hearts and knew
better than to let the dams break open.
so we kept working, we glanced, we pretended, and we
never spoke again.

what i didn't tell you then

was that i knew
i heard
i saw the path that would take us from nothing to
everything
i saw the hours of conversation that would thread our days
and the love that would inhabit our nights
i saw the softening, i saw the tenderness
i felt the strength, and the wisdom
the endless curiosity
the light in your smile,
and your eyes that could see
i heard the laughter that would become our refuge
and those arms forever intertwined
the good times, the bad times
the colors dancing
the music playing
the road trips
the wine
and the long walks
i knew it would take time
but i knew i was home.

ghosts

of a love past
inhabiting your space
and beauty all around
no part of you can taste
she's no longer there
but she is far from gone

smoke that fills your lungs
and numbs your every thought
as you lie awake
restless and afraid
beating on your heart
wishing things away

how is that working for you?

moments pass you by
magic as ever, glimpses of the new
promises of change
as you close your eyes
and waste the dream of you
and i shine my light
i stand in my might
i walk proud and tall
into a life i trust
as you toss and turn
as it slips you by
as it goes to dust

how is that working
for you?

whirlwinds and voices

chaos and old fears
the audience awaits
not sure i can do this

maybe i should cancel
breathe, i tell myself
it will calm the spinning
they'll love you she says
my heart still racing
my hands still shaking

vagal nerve grounding
prefrontal cortex out
no more room for doubt
as my feet slowly walk me to the stage
one last prayer and here we go

leap

and then

rapture.

bassam

the last time i saw him
it had been a while
he had aged
just a little bit
just enough to see
something new in his eyes
a little bit more of his old soul
perhaps getting ready to pack up and leave

the last time i saw him
he gave me a hug
i said i love you
and he held me close
i remember we laughed
perhaps a little softer
a little gentler
a little more humbly
than we had before
when things were good
when things were better
when we weren't sure yet
things would end this way

the last time i saw him
was an eternity ago,
where he is now
whispering in my ear
and reminding me
that love is all there is
and love never dies.

i own a ridiculous amount

of memories.

they come with me wherever i go. they're mostly
fun, sometimes not so much. they move around, they
transform. sometimes they grow, sometimes they fade.
they come in all shapes and sizes, sometimes through my
senses, and sometimes i feel them in my heart. fragrances,
colors, chocolate, kisses, sunsets. airports, clouds, hugs
and sometimes tears. but that's ok. tears deserve to be
remembered too. my worst memories were stuck in my
body for a long time, but now they've melted into softer
ones i can go over in my head every once in a while. they
travel with me as i learn and discover and experience. so
many millions of moments. threaded one way, and then
threaded another. and every day, i make more. and every
day, it's more fun to remember.
i love my memories so much. they're my favorite movie.

lost and found

a dark abyss
bottomless
years of looking
for who i thought i needed to become
uncovering every stone
every fear
taking every detour
loving every stranger
until it dawned on me
late one night
that i had been here all along

and now
i was never going to leave me again.

christiane

so tedious. not christine and not quite christiana. chris?
chrissy? christy? anything? so excruciating. what a
difference an A makes. why can't you just be christina like
everyone else? there's an A in there and we wouldn't have
to think. whose idea was this anyway? it's just a name and
it's the thought that counts. there, we gave it a whirl and
decided it was too complicated. chrissy it is and let's call it
a day.

i'm going to turn you into a short story

you just watch.

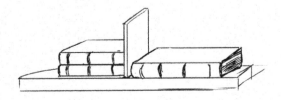

the swan

no one tells the story of the swan, who
upon finally joining her new found cast,
fought for her life to try and fit in
amongst her poised and noble peers.
forever haunted by her ugly duckling past
and all the darkness and fears
she now had to work even harder to conceal,
her truth forever tainted by a love that never came
and that she was now doomed to never know
how to receive.

forever an ugly duckling
trapped inside a swan
poised and noble,
kind and calm,
always shunned,
never quite living.

he couldn't possibly want me

of course he does. i am beautiful and whole and plenty. and a treasure to behold. i'm finally here, with all of me. i can't believe it took so long, but so good to at long last feel safe and joyous in the presence of love, for me, for him, for all that is.

yesterday i started feeling

ugly again.

something in the way he said what i'd heard him say so
many times before,
only different this time.
i didn't tingle with pleasure.
where was the thrill, why was there a hole in my heart
instead?
what was it that i heard? was it my fear?
or was it what he didn't have to say,
that filled the room with everything but magic,
and hung in the air as we attempted to dance
one last time?

eyes don't lie and i had turned into a pumpkin.

it was time to go.

7 pm

passed out in bed,
a ton of bricks thrust upon me,
a whisper of grief lurking
in my soul,
a lulling song that says
you have gone and it was all my fault.
all this love and nowhere to go
all these tears with no one to tell
all these years and nothing to show
all the words i wanted to say
vanquished in the vault,
held hostage by your fear and my fear.
you bowed to your fear, a tyrant
menacing and firm,
threatening to steal your joy
and all our tomorrows.
so many maybes and let's wait and sees,
have now crumbled to the ground,
drowned in the current,
lost at sea.
so much silence,
that is now making a deafening sound.
7pm, passed out in bed
a deafening song that says,
hush hush now, our love is dead.

ashes to ashes

rising strong,
babies crying,
twins and flames,
scattered away,
lifetimes and everything in between.
swaths of light and sound,
and reckoning in all ways,
southern mountains ,
holding hands,
children playing
and a love that never ends.

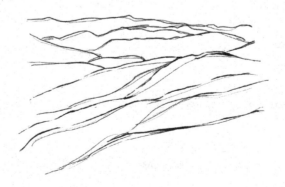

the good girl

in her

the ever quiet one, the one who saw everyone's pain but her own, wouldn't have said anything.

but she had learned, and finally knew to use her words, so she did.

and he left.

and she is going to be ok.

my mother's kitchen

was always full, hectic, brimming with meal plans. cabinets
and countertops were always bursting at the seams with
supplies. we never knew where the next ration would
come from so we had to be prepared. the refrigerators
tended to be empty, as we had no power and perishable
foods didn't stand a chance. the pantry was full of canned
goods and jars, so many jars. big jars, small jars, gigantic
this-is -more-than-you'll-need-in-a-lifetime jars.

but a lifetime felt so far away, so far removed from what
any of us imagined could ever be possible. i wonder what
those pickles would have to say, sitting in their jar years
later, had they survived the war. i wonder what stories
they would tell, about the spatter of blood on the shelf,
their fellow broken jars across from them, and the upstairs
neighbor who never got to finish his morning coffee that
day, sitting in his mother's kitchen, right above ours.

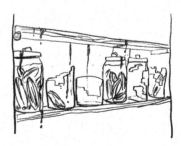

your lips

and i was home.

the party

we were going to gather, to celebrate the many birthdays
of the month. i was looking forward to a special night, it
was overdue, and we had not seen each other in a while.
there were so many milestones to commemorate and my
heart rejoiced at the tenderness ahead.
but there she was. and the silent vow of what was to
never change. a silence louder than the cheers and
birthday songs we sang. a contract stronger than any wish
i could've ever made. the ghost of their past, hovering
over my future. the time had come. life had taught me to
celebrate my solitude, and this year faithfully promised to
follow suit.

breathless

hellos and then goodbyes
gasping for air in between
counting the days, beating away
wondering
what mattered
what stayed
what formed
what lived
so many hellos,
and then goodbyes
and now sparser and sparser
more tears, more rapture
more joy impossible to capture
more packing up, more leaving
more maybe nots, less smiles
more miles
less kisses
more wistful memories
the ghost of a touch
still hovering
the shape of your lips
still haunting
another path
another time
but also
an exquisite story
unrepeatable
forever engraved
another gem to treasure
forever alive
two souls forever changed
for having dared to love.

younger

better.

stronger.

faster.

will i be annihilated because you exist? will i still have a
voice? do i still have a body, beaten, wounded, abused?
half healed and still in pain? while you can dance and
run and skip and bounce and outdance and outrun. me.
where do i stand now? can i even stand? does it even
matter if i stand at all. or live? or die? how do i come from
love, where do i even begin? how do we both win? you
came and it was over. too early. too bright. too light. i
didn't stand a chance. or was it life's way to show me i
would have to carve my own way? that i could carve my
own way? that my way was no one else's way? slow and
steady, fortitude laden. a warrior's path. an encourager's
pledge. i am getting there. and so are you, brighter and
lighter. but also thankful for the grounding of those who
came before you.

let's do this.
let us both win.

heaps of kisses

all those words we didn't speak,
heaps of kisses at the door,
wistful smiles
tossed amidst the piles,
of all the things that never were,
nor will ever now be.
off you go into the distance,
eyes on the road, ready to soar
off i go into myself
it will be a little while..
before i stop longing
for all the words we didn't speak.

heaps of kisses at the door,
soon autumn will be here
with many a new path to seek,
piles of you still on the floor
maybe in the morning..

turbulence

wait, what?
why am i shaking
heart is sinking
world is spinning
what was that post
what were those words
that never came
who is she?
where is he?
i need to sit down
or run, or call
or cry
i can't breathe
is anybody out there?
just stop the pain
please stop the pain
here's that movie again
the one where
everything is crashing
the one where
nothing is what i thought it was
the one where everyone lied
and i have been forgotten
again.

you and me

and a precipice

meet me where the stars dwell
and chains roll off our skins like
the freedom we'll never know.

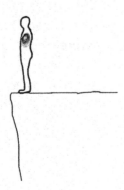

fall came early this year

with its leaves and its goodbyes
with its changing winds and winding roads
going nowhere my heart could follow

fall came early this year
and you were gone too soon
so many weeks, so many months
of so many moments imagined
but never lived
you were on your way
and the weeks and the months
skipped like chapters in a book
no one will ever read.
where did our summer go?
where did our moments go?
where did our road trips go
that we were going to take?
or was it just me hoping we would
asking that we would
wishing that we would?

but there was never time
too much to ponder
too much to regret
too much to pack
for us to ever have mattered at all
for us to ever have been anything at all
except a beautiful story
unlived and untold
a book we never even opened
and put right back on the shelf
as the leaves began to fall.

fall came early this year
and neither of us will ever know.

mitochondria

a microcosm. from my past, inviting me to take a look
back at how it all connects. while violence explodes
outside, bursts of anger, of unprocessed rage, of not
listening, of projectile vomiting of guilt and shame, my
insides calmly breathe and watch. so much abuse on
this body, mind, soul, heart, and decades of undoing
damage, grieving, and cleaning house so new life could
emerge. and now, forty years later, my cells are beginning
to rejoice. storms raging outside but they have learned to
dance in the rain.

guerres

tant de guerres
et puis ce tonnerre
qui gronde et qui menace en sourdine
tout le temps tout le temps tout le temps tout le temps
tout le temps tout le temps les tréfonds de cette guerre
où tout est englouti
les tréfonds du passé
la descente aux enfers
la monstrueuse machine où l'horreur vit encore
où la terreur survit malgré tant de lumière
la boîte ensevelie
au fond de ma pensée
dans les veines de mon corps
sous mes pas, dans mon lit
qui cache les âmes, les ruines, le sang et la ferraille
les cris, les tirs, les bombes et les brûlures
les rues, les mères, les tombes et les blessures
les tâches, la chair, les cendres et la mitraille
et mon coeur qui bat et qui bat

qui me bat, que je bats
et que je continue à battre
et qui continue de battre
malgré le poids et les larmes et la boîte et l'horreur
et la peur et les pleurs
et l'angoisse du pire et la faim de mourir malgré les cris et
mes cris
et l'envie de tout laisser et partir loin de cette bataille,
loin de la vie et loin de ma mise en terre
je ne veux plus de cette guerre.

peine

encore un jour se lève, se lève
encore un rêve de toi
le soleil brille, toujours, toujours
mais sans tes yeux, je ne vois pas
et ma peine, qui coule, qui coule
mon amour, est-ce que tu crois
à nos mains, à tous nos matins
qui n'attendent plus que toi

encore un jour s'achève, s'achève
tu es encore loin de moi
la nuit tombe, j'ai presque sommeil
mais dans mes yeux, je vois toi
dans mon coeur, qui coule, qui coule
mon amour, tu es là
et nos mains, et tous ces matins
éperdument, te disent.. viens!

épave

comment aimer une épave abandonnée par elle-même
une écorce de présence, une absence si présente
comment aimer dans le silence
des éléphants qui passent
et les relents d'alcool qui habitent tout ce que j'aime
comment aimer une image obscure et évasive
une idée, un amour, une illusion de vivre
comment continuer à oublier et à ne pas entendre
jour après jour tout ce qui n'est jamais dit
pourquoi aimer quand ça ne sert à rien
de se réveiller côte à côte tous les matins
de s'affairer à autre chose, à bien se surmener
et se rendormir le soir ensemble mais si lointains, chacun
tout seul dans son rêve emmuré
et ces relents d'alcool pour ne pas respirer?

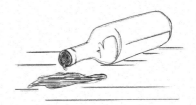

هلّأ فلّيت

لقيتك بلّيل، كان كلّو ليل، كان كلّو ويل
وإنت هون بهلّيل، هلّأ فلّيت
وقلبي كان ليل وكان كلّو ليل، كان كلّو ويل
وإنت هون بهلّيل، هلّأ فلّيت

يا حبيبي، حلمنا حلم، ولمّا صحينا
كان كلّوليل، كا كلّو ويل
راح ورجع الليل، هلّأ فلّيت

بتيجي على بالي

وكلّ شي تاني ما بعود بعود يعنيلي

لمّا تقرّب، تقرّب صوبي، كلّ شي بيوقف

كلّ شي بيوقف لمّا بتقعد حدّي

ليش لمّا بتحكيلي، كلّني بدوب

وصوتك قلبي بيعرف كلماتو

ليش لأ يا حبيبي، نحن هون، بكرا ما بينطر

ليش هل قدّ بتعنيلي، قلّي ليش هل قدّ بتعميني

إحساسي بقلّي ليش لأ هلّأ يا حبيبي، هلّأ حبّ

ليش لمّا بتيجي على بالي

كلّ شي تاني ما بعود بعود يعنيلي

قلّي ليش، بسّ تقرّب صوبي

قلبي بتتسرّع دقّاتو وبيسألك حبيبي، ليش، شو في بهدّني

كلّ هلّ إيّام هلّي عمبتمرؤ، صدفة ورا صدفة

ليش تنخلّي الصدفة، متكون إلّا صدفة

ما في شي موعود إلّا هلّيلة يا حبيبي..

91

حنين

نجوم إلّيل إلّيلة طلعت عبكّير

ودّمعة بقلبي الّيلة عم بتوجعني كتير

بعد شويّ بيطلع الضّوّ ، يا حزني طير

تركني بهمّي الّيلة شغلة وعم بتصير

ليل، آه، غيم، آه

ليل، آه، ويل، آه

آه، الحنين لقاني اليوم

وصور من الماضي على البال

لا كلام وبلا دموع

حنين بلقلب وسكوت وذكريات

نجوم إلّيل إلّيلة طلعت عبكّير

ودّمعة بقلبي رجع فيها حلم صغير

بعد شويّ بيطلع الضّو، وكلّ شي بصير

بكرا بيجي جايب معه حلم كبير

92

مين بقول

مين بيعرف ليش هون

ليش هلّأ تعرّفت عليك، وليش إيديك، وليش عينيك

نهار صيفيّة وشمس وصدفة

إيّام حنّيّة وشمس وخبار

ليالي نار، وخوفي طار

غمرني بقلبك يا حبيبي

ولا بعمرك تخلّيني روح

لو فيك تضّل حدّي عطول

thay

and as you went on
to inhabit bigger realms
the teachings continued to resound
with every step.
thank you
thank you
thank you,
teacher
master
loyal companion
ever present gifter
of all things kind
and true,
we love you.

about Christiane Karam

born and raised in war-torn Lebanon, Christiane Karam's eclectic vocal style stems from her love for different musical traditions. she has taught and performed around the world, and collaborated with the likes of Javier Limon, Tigran Hamasyan, Binka Dobreva and Bobby McFerrin, at venues such as Summerstage, Carnegie Hall and the Teatro Nacional to name a few. In addition to coaching and performing, she is an award-winning songwriter and the founder and leader of both the acclaimed Pletenitsa Balkan Choir and the Berklee Annual Middle Eastern Festival. she is currently on the faculty of Berklee College of Music where she continues her work of bringing awareness and positive social change through music and the arts. as a holistic practitioner, she is also committed to promoting wellness and balance through various mind-body practices.

for more info on Christiane Karam, please visit www.christianekaram.com